AF327229

SOME AMERICAN HISTORY

SOME AMERICAN HISTORY

Larry Rivers

Ellsworth Ausby

Peter Bradley

Frank Bowling

Daniel LaRue Johnson

Joe Overstreet

William Williams

introduced

by

Charles Childs

SOME AMERICAN HISTORY

Organized and circulated by the Institute for the Arts, Rice University
February 1971
Commissioned by the Ménil Foundation
Library of Congress Card Number 72-153088
Copyright © Institute for the Arts, Rice University Houston, Texas
Printed in West Germany by Philipp von Zabern, Mainz
New York Correspondent: S. W. Swan, 4 East 89 Street

SOME AMERICAN HISTORY

Film circulated

with the exhibition:

Slavery:

the black man

and the man

conceived

by

June Jordan

and

directed

by

John Chandler

SOME AMERICAN HISTORY

Ronald Hobbs participated in this project from the beginning. He discerned the pitfalls as well as the promises. He gave time and devotion helping dodge the first and boost the second.

Dominique de Ménil, director
Institute for the Arts
Rice University

LARRY OCEAN SWIMS THE NILE, MISSISSIPPI AND OTHER RIVERS

BY CHARLES CHILDS

In the turbulent dialectic of black peoples' drive to affirm their own cultural identity, the idea of having a white artist comment on black subject matter, on first glance, seems unacceptable.

Yet, one of the most famous artists of this generation, Larry Rivers, has pursued just this sort of endeavor and questions as to his intent and motivation say more about the "hang ups" in all of us than they do about just what, precisely, Larry Rivers is up to.

Basically separatist in its challenge, the whole idea of race purity and more qualified knowledge is just one more entrapment out of which the limitlessness of art will once again have to escape.

Nevertheless, the arrogance of artistic freedom, to someone who has yet to achieve equality, may be what prompted one black critic to hurl the slur, "Great White Father, Larry Ocean" at Rivers in an article that raised, as a result of its undiscerning narrowness, serious questions about "cultural privacy" and the new rule of "Apartheid" that says only blacks can interpret blackness.

That such ideas are understandable in view of the inaccurate projection of black identity in American history is obvious. Still, the arbitrary nature of ignorance so characteristic of white oppression, turned back on whites, in no way can be interpreted as black perception or intelligence, much less black pride.

On the contrary, throughout all the levels of black life in America, despite the rhetoric of "nationhood" and "self-determination," much to the credit and subtlety of black understanding, there have been certain exceptional whites who have been accepted. These whites, some of whom have walked in the footprints of John Brown, who have died beside black brothers in the struggle for human dignity, find acceptance not out of a feeling that they are "special" but rather out of an awareness that distinguishes individuals on merit and the deeper knowledge that sympathetic and constructive work by whites, ready to correct the record and reveal the truth about history, can complement black aspirations.

All this, of course, brings us to the case in point: Larry Rivers, a sort of peg in a square hole, who is neither as lily white, say, as Norman Rockwell nor as wasplike as Andrew Wyeth . . . but who really in full measure has his own thing going for him.

Curiously enough, being neither lily white nor lamp black, but between two worlds, is the merit of Larry Rivers. In a certain way, it means he can be anything, assimilate anything. Consequently, if his curiosity about the energy and vitality of another culture has made him a trespasser, it is because he sees racial boundaries as essentially contrived and ultimately untenable and, being true to his unbridled spirit, he wants to leap over walls, especially those that separate men from each other.

Actually, Rivers, who in 1967 traveled 10,000 miles throughout Africa, is a seasoned traveler, not a first time tourist; and now his exhibition SOME AMERICAN HISTORY, with all its concentration on the one theme of race, is really only one of a series of glimpses into black experience that Rivers has taken over the years that span, incredibly enough, nearly a quarter of a century of art production.

Take for example a painting commissioned by the Container Corporation of America in 1964. Here, Rivers ventured into the black world with courage and candor. Juxtaposing a black woman against the idealized image of the *Ebony* magazine skin-lightened example, Rivers, in his *The Identification Manual*, took on the ghastly and incriminating subject of false beauty standards as imposed by a self-denigrating black mass media magazine. Shocking and revealing in its directness, The *Identification Manual*, coming at a time when "black is beautiful" had not surfaced, was forcefully remarkable in both its perception and accuracy.

10

Here in this early show of brilliance, Rivers goes beyond identification with blacks on a compassionate and liberal level. Instead, he enters the alien world with an integrity that gets to the "nitty grit" of an issue where the truth can sometimes be as embarrassing and as penetrating as an unbridled fart, blurted out into the open.

Historically, other white artists trespassing the boundaries of black life through art have not been as accurate. In literature, Harriet Beecher Stowe's examination of slave attitudes in *Uncle Tom's Cabin*, for example, proved to be a patronizing distortion despite Miss Stowe's anti-slavery benevolence. Later, fortunately, Mark Twain modified this rendering of "Uncle Tom" in his sympathetic depiction of "Jim" who chooses to run away, Eldridge Cleaver style, rather than stay and dance to "white folks music."

The same distortion and correction occurs to a significant degree in American paintings of the 1800's. Beginning with the burlesque of black life depicted in the Currier & Ives *Darktowns* series and the deification of the "good nigger" typified in Eastman Johnson's *Old Kentucky Home* paintings.

Not until the arrival of the Ashcan School, exemplified in the work of George Bellows and Thomas Eakins, teacher to the famous black painter Henry O. Tanner, were black subjects given prominence and sympathy.

Winslow Homer, for one, was among the first to get away from the old minstrel-show conception in order to portray black experience with truth and understanding. Homer, who lived at times in Nassau in the Bahamas, was quick to recognize the strength and beauty of West Indian blacks. His painting, *Gulf Stream*, depicting a Bahamian black lying on the deck of a dismasted boat surrounded by sharks, waiting for inevitable death as an oblivious ship passes in the distance, drawing the condition and paranoia of black experience in a way that has yet to be duplicated in today's art — black or white.

Other humanizing views, such as James Chapin's heroic *Ruby Green Singing*, the grim reality of Reginald Marsh's *Why Not Use The El?*, and Ben Shahn's *Willis Avenue Bridge* depicting the stamina and strength of black existence even in old age, exemplify the ways in which white American artists were able to update and identify with the image of black life in America and, more often than not, express their resentment at the injustice inherent in it.

In tackling the vastness of black life and history in this tradition, Larry Rivers brings to the subject his unique proximity to the black community, and his tendency to draw on this "intimacy" to make art of his own life.

"Black life to me is a whole spectrum of people I've met and come to know at various times," Rivers admits. "It is a perception of race and culture with as many variables and dimensions as people are variable. Because of some of these people, I think I've become sensitized, enriched and broadened. After all," Rivers continues, "more than being an artist, I am a political man. I am affected by what other men do and say and think and what I have produced as an artist is my relationship to other men which points out our differences and our similarities."

Consequently, Rivers, always social, never closes himself off from new contacts and new experiences. His life is the happening of a dozen or more important chance occurrences that would not have flowered had he not been open to assimilation.

By chance, for instance, after his discharge from the Air Force in 1943, Rivers, who earned his living around New York as an accomplished jazz musician, happened to fall into a friendship with a musician whose wife happened to be an artist. She introduced him to Nell Blaine, a New York painter, who happened to suggest that he study with the great, now deceased, Hans Hoffmann.

Prior to this period, Rivers had tiptoed on the fringes of the black world and had it not been for his interest in essentially non-white music, the music of Charlie Parker and Lester Young, he might never have made the contacts that eventually encouraged him to be an artist.

It was really this appetite for another culture that lured him beyond the confines of his middle class Bronx, New York Jewish family.

12

A roustabout hipster, Rivers gravitated to the opposite of "square" Bar-Mitzvah-type upbringing, not out of disrespect for his own Jewishness, but, here again, because of his insatiable curiosity concerning the world around him. Like the white prototype of Norman Mailer's "white-negro," Rivers paid his acculturation dues in all-night rent parties in Harlem and got his first short-sighted impressions of black life through intimate associations with pimps, street hustlers and one special whore who took him home to meet her family.

But there were other more devastating, less romanticized insights into the inequities that exist for those who are black in America.

"My father had this business," Rivers remembers, "he had black guys working for him and one day it suddenly hit me that he was paying them peanuts. When he would meet any of the men on the street, I noticed that he would act kind of slaphappy, in a way that he wasn't prior to that moment . . . you know, like they were children. Once all hell broke loose because my sister brought this black guy home. My mother made a fuss and it struck me as the biggest contradiction in the world that a Jewish lady should make a fuss, since that was precisely the kind of shit we put Hitler down for."

These are the sort of contradictions against which Larry Rivers has used his art. His frankness has always verged on the edge of rebellion, simply because he hates hypocrisy. When his family eventually came to figure in his work, he painted them without faces in *The Burial* and *Bar-Mitzvah*. Later, in the now famous painting of his mother-in-law, *Double Portrait of Birdie*, Rivers publicized her flawed and aged nakedness in almost cruel, unabashed realism.

A compulsive urge to truth, which means truth first denied but deeply felt in spite of itself, is a recurring motif in the work of Larry Rivers. It is this successful working through to where it's really at, this victory over himself that is the most corrosive. Consequently, what everybody knows as the normal and ordinary visual cliché, once turned upside down and laid bare by Rivers, can often prove unnerving. Perhaps this accounts for why some critics see the flamboyance of Larry Rivers as a kind of comic weakness, when

13

actually, in a way, the free admission of his own banality, the banality epitomized in *Lamp Man Loves It*, whereby a 7-foot black man achieves vivid connection with a complacent friend by way of a flashing lightbulb, belongs to a whole area of emotional and intellectual conquests.

There were many blacks, as well as many whites, who could not accept *Lamp Man Loves It*. An art dealer gave credence to the belief that the art world is blatantly racist by his initial displeasure with the explicit depiction of a black man and white woman in sexual communication. "He kept suggesting that I should show the face unfinished, so Lamp Man's race would not be noticeable," Rivers reports.

Only Rivers, true to his renegade nature, finally altered the piece, so that on exhibition, the girl now looked oddly like a man, throwing up the theme of homosexuality for those preoccupied with art as only a serious "priggish" exposition.

For this and many other scandalous reasons, Larry Rivers is constantly being accused of not taking art seriously, of being capricious. His tendency to unvarnish and disembody hallowed images is more a part of his inheritance than he is willing to admit. A significant remnant of his Jewishness, this tendency toward wit and humor in his work is a particular view of reality that has historical roots in the treadmill and banana peel of minority group status. In Jewish wit, it is the ability to be uncompromising, to laugh at oneself sympathetically, through the pathos of the "meshuggana" and the "schlemiel," in much the same way as Langston Hughes' character "Simple" analyzes the futility and irony that come from carrying an oppressor's burden.

In SOME AMERICAN HISTORY, however, Rivers was careful not to give the wide range of his comic tendency irresponsible freedom. "You can make fun about something which is already established, an institution or a fact in past history," Rivers acknowledged, "but here with this exhibition, I had to take into account that black history is still being made, and rather than evaluate that history, I wanted to simply reveal some of the conditions out of which it is still evolving."

14

Such an ambitious notion seemed overwhelming to Rivers at the outset. He knew he wanted to set out on a journey into blackness, but it was territory he had only partially charted. For this reason, he was not adverse to accepting instruction. Unlike the questionable exhibit, *Harlem On My Mind*, with its Cotton Club title, presented in 1969 at New York's Metropolitan Museum of Art over the protest of blacks who wanted some say in the exhibition's production, Rivers sought and received help and contributions from black artists.

True to his tradition that subjectifies and personalizes everything, Rivers ignored the more established black artists, collaborating only with "cats," as he calls them, who were friends and whose work he knew and admired.

"My decisions and choices come out of a combination of laziness, social contacts, accidents and what I'm impressed by," he admits. "I knew this girl who worked at the Schomberg Collection in Harlem. Together we went to bookshops, gathering a lot of material on black history. As I digested this material, I tested my knowledge with people like Frank Bowling and other black friends and acquaintances."

It was through Frank Bowling, a black painter who is actually a Guyanese by nationality, that Larry Rivers eventually made contact with several other black artists. "When I told them I was going to do a show on black subject matter," Rivers recalls, "they looked at me as if I was a nut. So, I said, why not contribute something . . . a painting, a sculpture, anything; and they said, what are you — some kind of hip overseer? I said no, that I didn't think you had to be a chicken to talk about an egg, but that I was acknowledging their special expertise. Ya know, how they were chickens."

In this casual manner, six black painters, Daniel Johnson, Peter Bradley, William Williams, Frank Bowling, Joe Overstreet and Ellsworth Ausby, made up the collective that would later produce SOME AMERICAN HISTORY. "An exhibition which could be seen as one piece composed of a lot of pieces,"Rivers theorized.

The consequences of this inclusion of black artists into SOME

AMERICAN HISTORY is the obvious extension of group seeing over individual perception. Where Rivers falls short as the result of being "Ofay," and this is seldom, others in the exhibition bring the concerns of artistic expression to the wellsprings of innermost black feeling.

Actually, the idea for the exhibition, being the overriding vision of Larry Rivers himself by way of a commission, is unprecedented. No artist with a similar commission has ever opened it up to include the works of other artists. But Rivers, true to his life style, often a gobbledygook of disjointed fragments, cannot resist expanding experience, much less extending invitations.

In contrast to today's minimal abstractionists with their rather severe structural fastidiousness, Rivers debunks the whole notion that more is less; instead, he favors the very human idea that more is more. Anybody, anything and anyone can get into the act. In fact, as writer Bob Reisner claims, even common everyday doodles such as graffiti, a form of underground communication between anonymous man and his world, can also make sort of off the wall contributions.

Borrowing this idea, Rivers incorporated wall writing into his 1964 set for the Imamu Baraka (LeRoi Jones) one-act play *The Toilet*. It is a leitmotif carried over into much of his work and there are few of his paintings that do not have some of this inclination to scribble and write over the surfaces of them. In SOME AMERICAN HISTORY, Rivers graphically illustrates this sense of anonymous communication through the words *Du Bois Died In Ghana*, hand scrawled as if by a revolutionary.

The inspiration for this is a direct lift from the kind of revolutionary wall writing seen in New York subways. In its secrecy, this slogan *Du Bois Died In Ghana* provides just the right underground voice feeling for the ironic, almost subversive message that a great black American chose to live outside America, rather than in it.

Techniques such as these, the use of everyday folklore and public language of the street, the symbols and signs in store windows, on automobiles and photographs, all and everything typical of an urban

16

environment, have put Rivers one step ahead of the pop generation. Ahead of his time as early as 1955, Rivers was putting the American flag as well as commercial objects into his paintings and this, in a way that has now given rise to "flag art" among hippies and, unfortunately, hardhats also.

This characteristic to incorporate still holds true for Rivers as he explains how Some American History took shape, "from a series of spontaneous interactions with endless troops of friends and associates."

Such incorporation of "friendly ideas" can be seen in one of the most important set pieces of the Some American History exhibit, *Lynching*.

"The idea was a blockbuster," Rivers remembers. "It grew out of a SNCC picture I had seen showing a lynching and a lot of white guys standing around smiling. At first I wanted to reproduce that situation. So, I chose to work in 3-dimension rather than canvas to make the event come alive. I made plywood figures and strung them up in my studio. James Haskins, the black writer who wrote *Diary of a Harlem Schoolteacher*, stopped by and looked behind each of the figures. He said, 'Oh, I thought there would be a white chick on the reverse side.' I took this to mean the idea was incomplete without the chick, so I put her on the floor underneath the figures, to emphasize the sexual inference under the issue of race in this country."

This capacity to go beyond completeness, to state precisely what art exhibitions normally don't state, is perhaps the most significant by-product of Some American History.

Here are the hidden ideas that blacks feel and whites know, but that racism in America dictates should never be mentioned, out in the open; as they are in the work, *New Jemima*, by Joe Overstreet.

Overstreet, who normally paints in a non-figurative genre nevertheless departs from his usual style in a work which borrows the benevolent figure of Aunt Jemima from the familiar box of pancake flour. Flipflopping this image, Overstreet gives us a new and more volatile Aunt Jemima. "How many older black women must have resented this image," Overstreet explains. "How many had to play that role just to sneak home some food for their children? I wanted to say that now those children are grown, and that the old image of Aunt Jemima, unless things change drastically, can erupt into a whole new personality."

Shattering stereotypes in a similar manner, artist Danny Johnson departs from his normally abstract sculpture making to vent his response through the total realism of his large work, *Over Here, Over There.*

"This is a work," Johnson says, "that speaks for itself. It shows how black women in history have nursed white children, and how now you have only to look around to see white girls nursing black children. It says if you want some milk and you're a baby, you can go over there and get some and you can go over here and get some, which is just another way of saying that the lines dividing people are just a lot of bull."

While artists William Williams and Peter Bradley keep to less literal and more abstract responses to the theme of the exhibition, most of the artists contributing can be said to align with the tendency of the exhibit to pull away from abstraction.

By implication, this would seem to suggest that the communication of theme material may have something to do with method, especially when it comes to handling subject matter fraught with socio-political overtones.

Still, despite the usual fear that accompanies socially reflective art and the stigma (no less than racist) that has been particularly acute for black artists, one which accuses them of being sociologists if they paint black subject matter and not "savage" enough if they adopt white mannerisms, the attempt to resolve statement and estheticism in SOME AMERICAN HISTORY has been achieved.

Accomplishments along these lines can be seen in the work of Frank

Bowling, the Guyanese artist whose large work, *The Middle Passage,* combines the map forms of Africa, America and Guyana into an autobiographical frame, where stenciled iconographs seem to haunt the work like ghosts.

Strongly disciplined by intellectualized beliefs, Bowling feels that painting must always be primarily art before it is statement. "I named the painting *Middle Passage,*" he said, "because I am a product of the middle passage. But what is significant is the fact that I do not bring my images together because of the history and brutality of that terrible crossing, but rather in spite of it."

Equally grudging on this issue of keeping art out of the earthbound dungeons of cold, topical journalism is the characteristic, unprogrammatic way Larry Rivers approaches a subject. Inspired directly by what visually excites him, Rivers improvises out of a variety of materials that span a range from painting to makeshift carpentry.

Stoop, for instance, a 3-dimensional work originally conceived as a piece that might depict the squalor of a ghetto environment, turns out to be more monumental than it is seamy. Constructed of wood and having the ambiance of an Egyptian sphinx, *Stoop* is the embodiment of Rivers' appetite for flourish on a grand scale; the kind of sweeping grandeur he gives to another wood constructed work, *Slave Ship.*

Magnificently appointed with its large expanse of sail and langorous jigsaw fashioned waves, *Slave Ship* has none of the chilling grimness, the iron shackles and wall-to-wall crowding one usually associates with the Atlantic crossing: here, Rivers, true to his artistic instincts, cannot help but transmute a truth, especially one which is not beautiful, into an art that is.

But where Rivers misrepresents history for the sake of art, he vindicates himself by spotlighting history on its own raw terms. This, Rivers accounts for with his numerous and authentic "documentary notes" spotted throughout the exhibition; some in the form of prints and writings that in their unadulterated presence bear witness to the past.

One such work, which can be said to have been raised to the status of
art, just by dint of being rescued from oblivion, is an old print en-
titled *Returning Burns*.

Poignant in its literal translation of a real event out of history,
Returning Burns tells of the ordeal of a runaway slave: "On Friday,
when Burns was sentenced to return to slavery twenty-two military
units including the entire Fifth Regiment of Artillery, were assembled in Boston to see that Burns did not escape and a cannon
was set up in front of the courthouse. Beside the police of Boston,
1,500 dragoons, marines and lancers, with Burns in their midst,
marched to the dockside through streets lined by a crowd of 50,000
persons hissing and crying, 'Shame!'"

These then are a few of the themes and people who make up SOME
AMERICAN HISTORY, an exhibition conceived by Larry Rivers as a
forum for visual communication where, finally, in these times of
confusion and racial mistrust, art and political man are both com-
mented upon and reconciled.

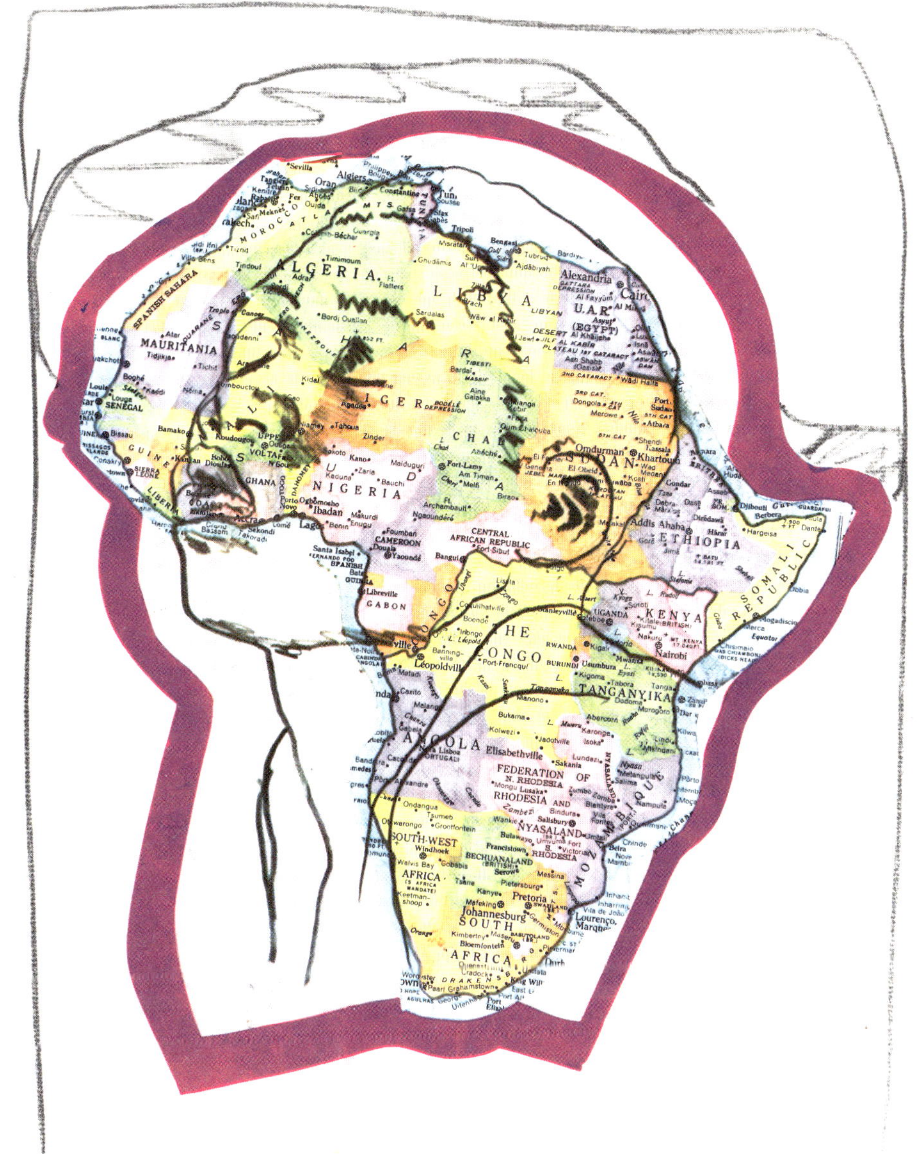

MOROCCO
SPANISH SAHARA
MAURITANIA
ALGERIA
LIBYA
U.A.R. (EGYPT)
LIBYAN DESERT
SENEGAL
MALI
NIGER
CHAD
SUDAN
NIGERIA
GHANA
UPPER VOLTA
DAHOMEY
CAMEROON
SPANISH GUINEA
GABON
CENTRAL AFRICAN REPUBLIC
ETHIOPIA
SOMALI REPUBLIC
CONGO
THE CONGO
RWANDA
BURUNDI
UGANDA
KENYA
TANGANYIKA
ANGOLA (PORTUGAL)
FEDERATION OF RHODESIA AND NYASALAND
N. RHODESIA
S. RHODESIA
MOZAMBIQUE
SOUTH-WEST AFRICA (S. AFRICA MANDATE)
BECHUANALAND (BRITISH)
SOUTH AFRICA
Alexandria
Cairo
Khartoum
Omdurman
Addis Ahaba
Nairobi
Léopoldville
Luanda
Elisabethville
Windhoek
Johannesburg
Pretoria
Bloemfontein
Algiers
Oran
Tripoli
Bengasi
Lagos
Ibadan
Bamako

3

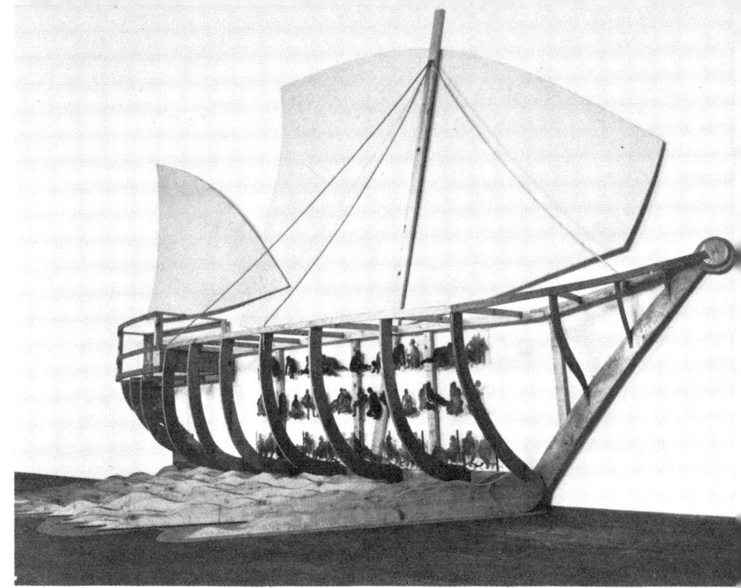

5 *(detail following page)*

About twenty persons were seized in our village at the time I was; and amongst these were three children so young they were not able to walk or to eat any hard substance. The mothers of these children had brought them all the way with them and had them in their arms when we were taken on board this ship.

When they put us in irons to be sent to our place of confinement in the ship, the men who fastened the irons on these mothers took the children out of their hands and threw them over the side of the ship into the water.

quoted from *A Narrative of the Life and Adventures of Charles Ball, A Black Man,* by Charles Ball (1854) (J. Lester, *To Be A Slave* [New York: The Dial Press, 1968], pp. 24-25)

This picture of a poor fugitive is from one of the stereotypes manufactured in this city, for the southern market, and used on handbills offering rewards for runaway slaves.

THE RUNAWAY.

Kono bearded mask. Guinea

A group of captives being taken to the coast for sale as slaves.

9

Thomas Sims in court.

Before dawn some 300 armed constables gathered at the courthouse to escort Sims to a southbound ship while a crowd of abolitionists cried shame upon the city of Boston. At the dockside they sang hymns and prayed. In many churches bells tolled as the young Negro was carried back into bondage. In a speech about the Sims case, Wendell Phillips, the non-resistant, for the first time indicated approval of the use of violence. "It is just possible that the fugitive slave, taking his defense in his own right hand, and appealing to the first principle of natural law, may . . . gain the attention of all, and force them to grapple with the problem of slavery and the Fugitive Slave Bill." And Garrison added, "Every fugitive slave is justified in arming himself for protection and defense."

10

Boston police guarding Sims.

II

I2

e courthouse during Sims' trial.

$40,000
for a Slave

When on May 24, 1854, Anthony Burns was arrested and placed under guard in the federal jury room of the Boston courthouse at the behest of his former master, Colonel Charles Suttle of Alexandria, Virginia, the news spread quickly although an attempt was made to keep it secret. The next morning three distinguished lawyers were in court to defend him: Charles M. Ellis, a member of the Boston Vigilance Committee the purpose of which was to protect the rights of colored persons; Richard Henry Dana, Jr., author of *Two Years Before the Mast*; and Robert Morris, the city's most prominent colored attorney.

The following evening Faneuil Hall was filled to overflowing with citizens gathered to protest Burns' arrest and to denounce the posse sworn in as special constables to guard him, nearly a third of whom were known thugs with prison records. On the platform of Faneuil Hall that night, after Wendell Phillips and Theodore Parker had spoken, a man cried, "When we go from this Cradle of Liberty, let us go to the tomb of liberty—the courthouse!" The crowd broke for Court Square, where the Reverend Thomas Wentworth Higginson and Lewis Hayden were already leading a group of abolitionists in battering down the door of the courthouse to rescue Burns. But within, constables and deputies were ready with pistols and clubs. Reverend Higginson was wounded and in the scuffle one of the deputies was killed. Military reinforcements arrived, the abolitionists were routed and many were arrested.

Despairing of freeing Burns by force or by legal means, over the weekend the friends of freedom raised $1,200 and negotiated to purchase his freedom. But the U.S. Attorney refused to permit this transaction, insisting that in keeping with the Fugitive Slave Law the refugee must be returned to Virginia.

When Burns came to trial on Monday police and soldiers surrounded the courthouse, guarded every door and window and lined the staircase leading to the courtroom. From Washington, President Pierce wired to spare no expense in having the military protect the court "to insure execution of the law."

On Friday, when Burns was sentenced to return to slavery twenty-two military units, including the entire Fifth Regiment of Artillery, were assembled in Boston to see that Burns did not escape and a cannon was set up in front of the courthouse. Besides the police of Boston, 1,500 dragoons, marines and lancers, with Burns in their midst, marched to the dockside through streets lined by a crowd of 50,000 persons hissing and crying, "Shame!" At one point, the populace tried to break through a police cordon and rescue Burns. Several were injured. As the revenue cutter *Morris* sailed for Virginia that day with Burns aboard, the Reverend Daniel Foster ordered the crowd on the dock to kneel in prayer.

Although the slave's market value was only $1,200, it had cost the government more than $40,000 to return Anthony Burns to his master. "We rejoice," wrote the Richmond *Enquirer*, "but a few more such victories and the South is undone."

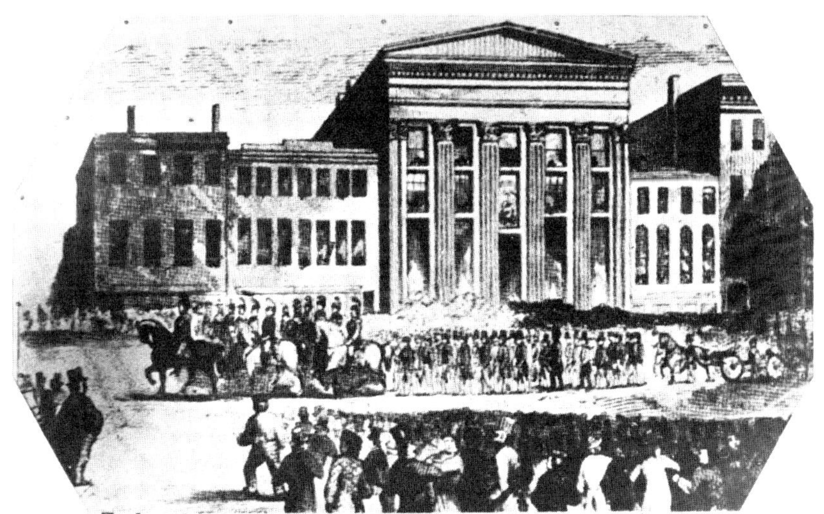

Federal
and state troops returning Burns to slavery.

16

18

N.Y.
ILL.
O.
W.V.
KY.
TENN.
MISS.
ALA.

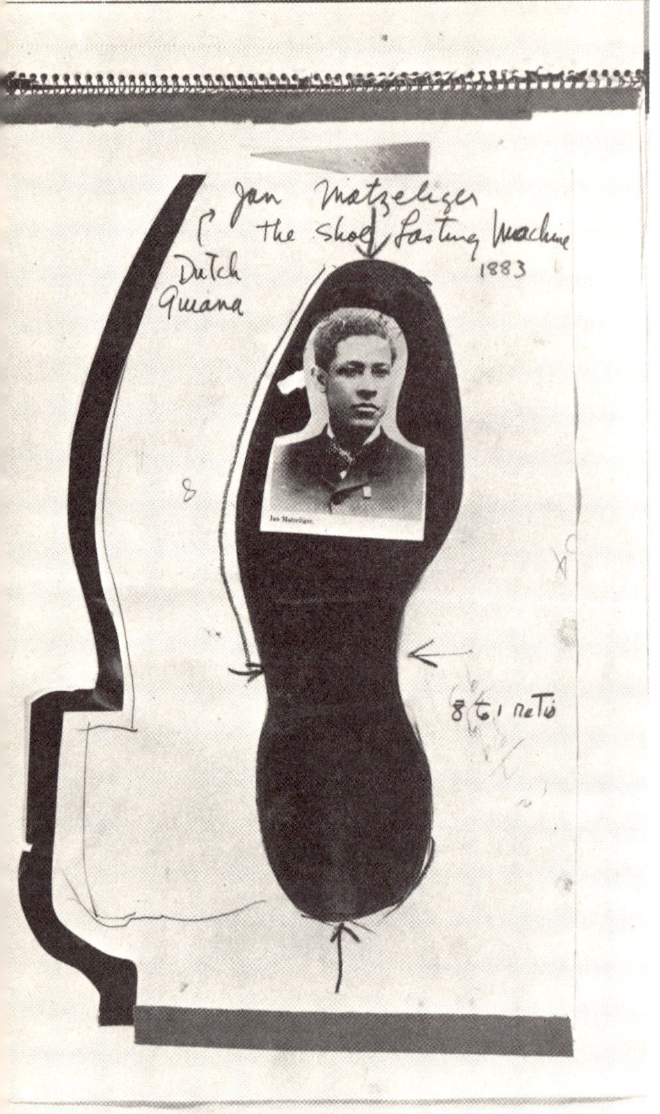
Jan Matzeliger
the shoe lasting machine
1883
Dutch
Guiana
Jan Matzeliger.
8½ to 1 ratio

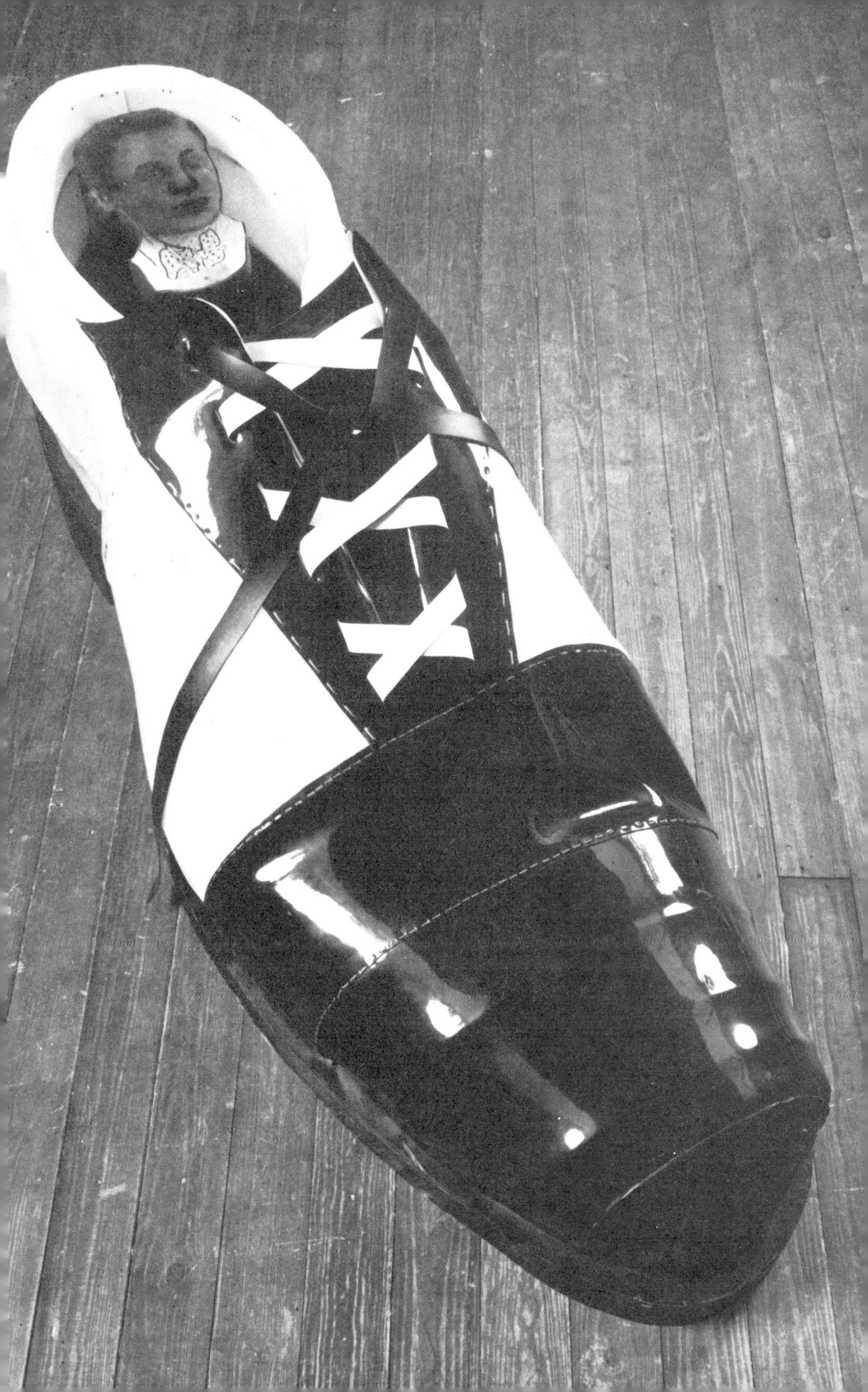

SHREVEPORT, La., Apr. 9 — Tom Miles, a negro, aged 29,
was hanged to a tree here and his body filled with
bullets early today. He had been tried in police court
yesterday on a charge of writing insulting notes to a white
girl, employed in a department store, but was acquitted
for lack of proof.

MONTGOMERY ADVERTISER
April 10, 1912
(R. Ginzburg, *100 Years of Lynching*
[New York: Lancer Books, 1969], p. 76)

22

Mrs.

Florida

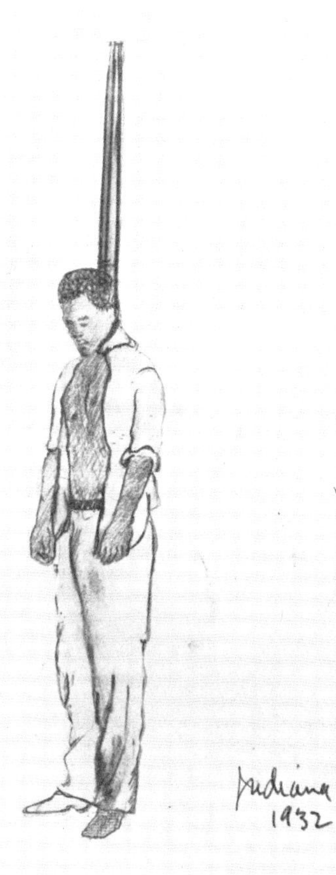

Indiana
1932

Indiana
1932

DU BOIS
DIED IN GHANA

We will not be satisfied to take one jot or tittle less than
our full manhood rights. We claim for ourselves every
single right that belongs to a freeborn American:
political, civil, social; and until we get these rights,
we will never cease to protest and assail the ears of
America. The battle we wage is not for ourselves alone,
but for all true Americans.

W. E. B. Du Bois

Present day statesmen are making the biggest blunder of the age if they believe that there can be any peace without equity and justice to all mankind.

Marcus Garvey

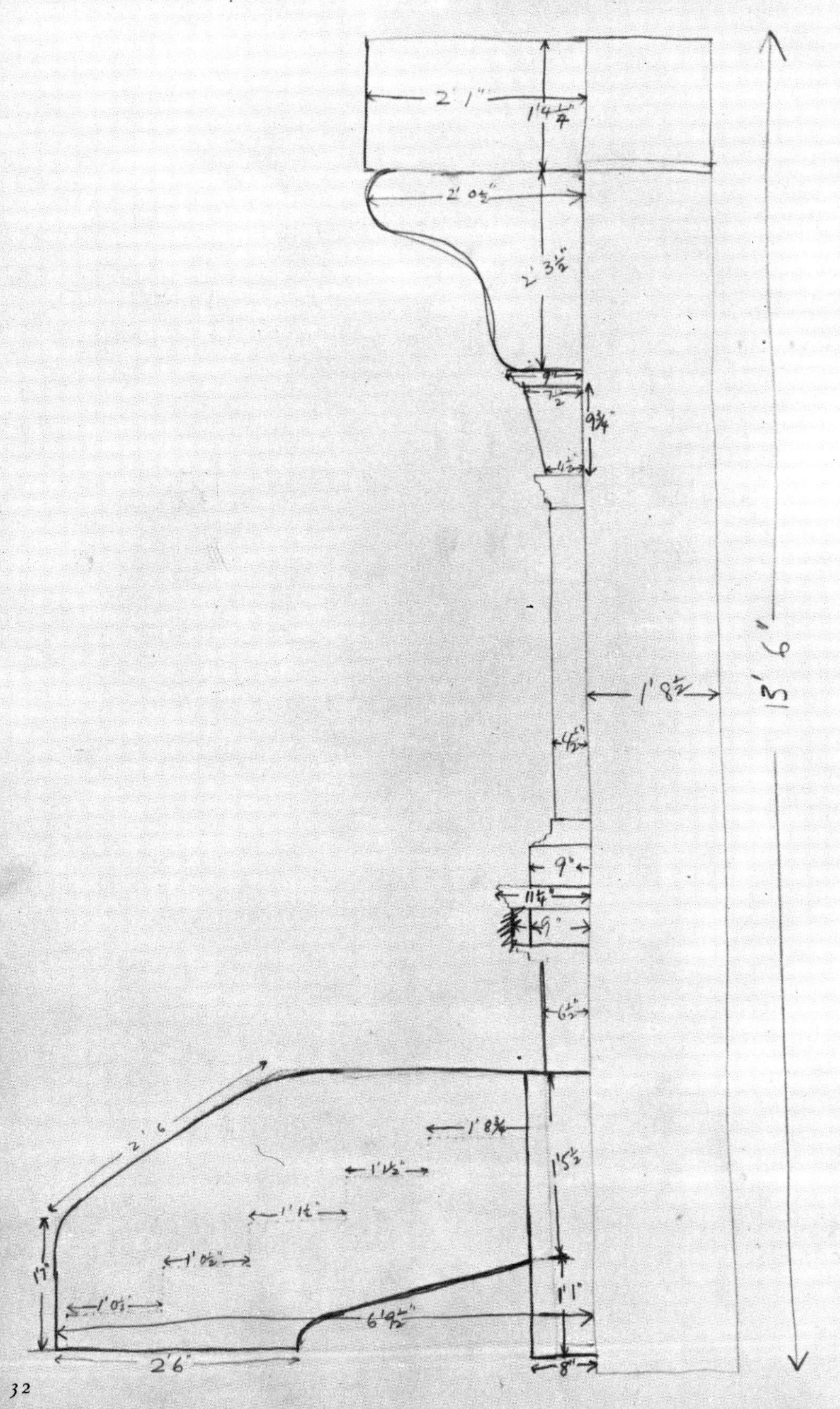
2' 1"
1' 4 1/4"
2' 0 1/2"
2' 3 1/2"
7 1/2"
9 3/4"
4 1/2"
1' 8 1/2"
4 1/2"
9"
11 1/4"
9"
6 1/2"
3' 6"
1' 8 3/4"
1' 1 1/2"
1' 1 1/2"
2' 6
1' 0 1/2"
1' 5 1/2"
1"
1' 0 1/2"
6' 0 1/2"
1' 1"
2' 6"
8"
32

35

We're all in the same boat and we are all going to catch
the same hell from the same man. He just happens to be
a white man. All of us have suffered here, in this country,
political oppression at the hands of the white man,
economic exploitation at the hands of the white man,
and social degradation at the hands of the white man.

Now in speaking like this, it doesn't mean that we're
anti-white, but it does mean that we're anti-exploitation,
we're anti-degradation, we're anti-oppression. And if the
white man does not want us to be anti-him, let him stop
oppressing and exploiting and degrading us.

Malcolm X

FIVE PLAYS
BY ED
BULLINS

GEORGE WASHINGTON CARVER

CROSSING THE DUPONT RIVER

MAY 17, 1954

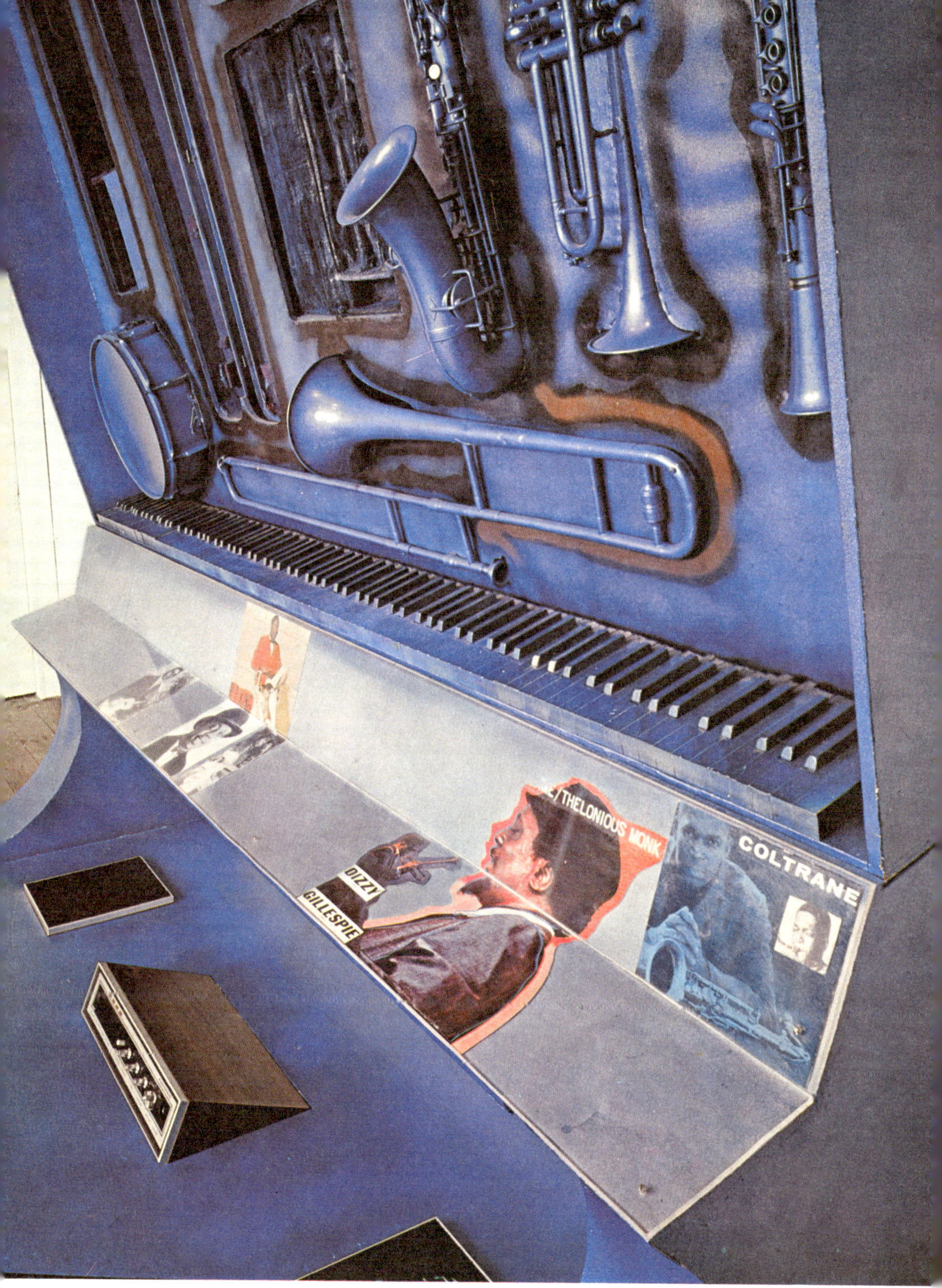

/THELONIOUS MONK
COLTRANE
DIZZY
GILLESPIE

45¢ 1ST 1/6 MILE
10¢ EACH ADD'L 1/6 MILE

41

40

The young whites know that the colored people of the
world, Afro-Americans included, do not seek revenge for
their suffering. They seek the same things the white
rebel wants: an end to war and exploitation.

Eldridge Cleaver

E
R
G
I
L
A

RED
BLUE

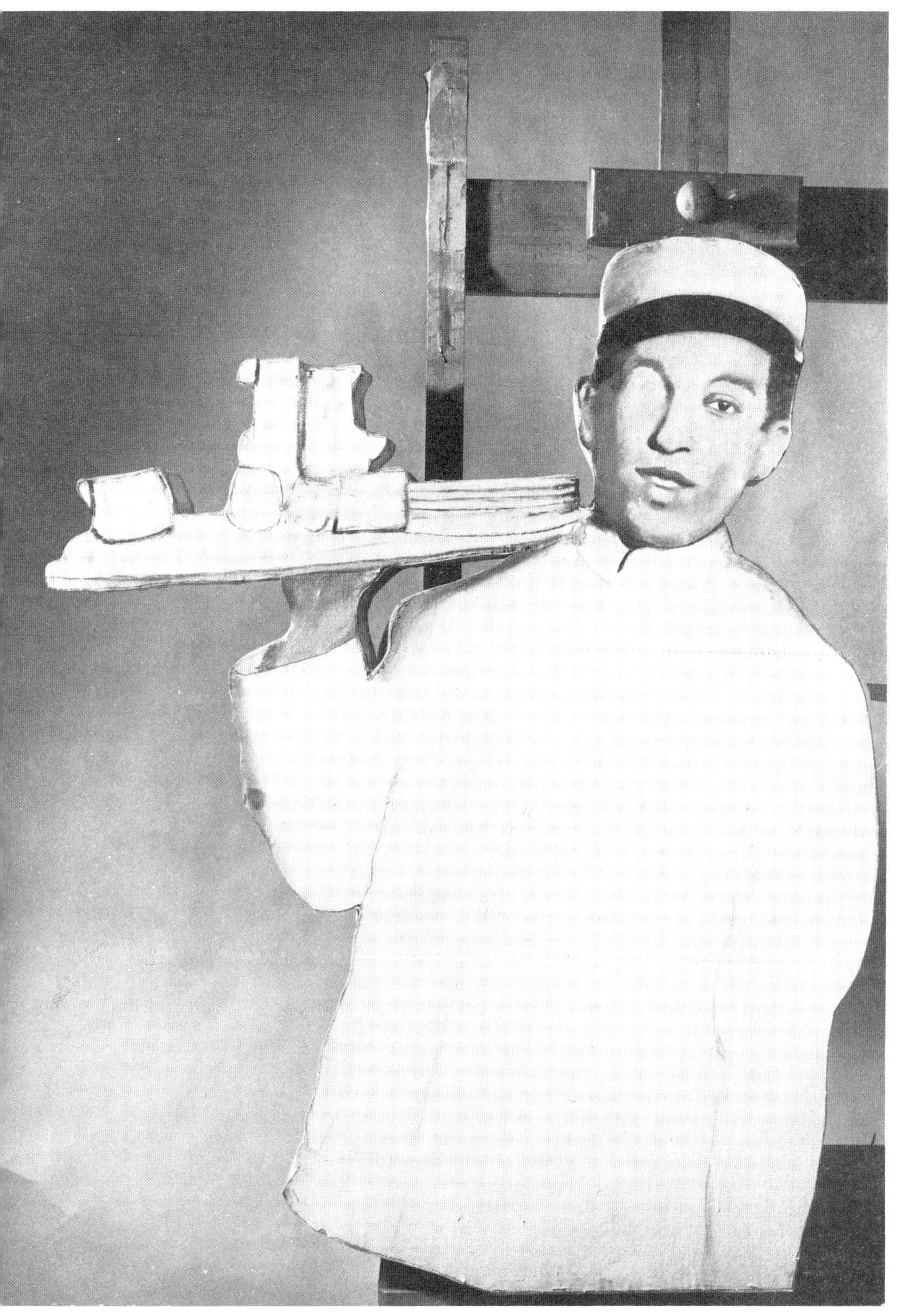

MADE IN U.S.A
NEW
JEMIMA

LISTING

1. RIVERS. *Africa Collage*, 1969. Mixed media. H: 17 1/2" (44.4 cm.); W: 12" (30.5 cm.).

2. RIVERS. *Africa Collage* (silver and mauve), 1969. Mixed media. H: 17 1/2" (44.4 cm.); W: 12" (30.5 cm.). Not illustrated.

3. RIVERS. *Slave Market*, 1969-70. Mixed media. H: 13 7/8" (35.3 cm.); W: 16 7/8" (42.9 cm.).

4. RIVERS. *Slave Market*, 1969-70. Mixed media. H: 10 1/2" (26.7 cm.); W: 14 1/2" (36.8 cm.). Not illustrated.

5. RIVERS. *A Slave Ship and Slaves*, 1970. Construction. H: 13 1/2' (411.5 cm.); W: 22' (670.6 cm.). D: 54" (137.2 cm.).

6. RIVERS. *Slave Ship*, 1969. Pencil on paper. H: 19" (48.3 cm.); W: 21 5/8" (55.6 cm.). Not illustrated.

7. RIVERS. *Eight Slaves*, 1970. Mixed media. Each, H: 17" (43.2 cm.); W: 14" (35.6 cm.).

8. RIVERS. *Panel: Runaway Slaves*, 1970. H: 60" (152.4 cm.); W: 36" (91.4 cm.).

9. RIVERS. *Panel: Caution — Colored People*, 1970. H: 48" (121.9 cm.); W: 24" (61 cm.).

10. RIVERS. *Panel: Sims*, 1970. H: 48" (121.9 cm.); W: 18" (45.7 cm.).

11. RIVERS. *Panel: Boston Police Guarding Sims*, 1970. H: 36" (91.4 cm.); W: 24" (61 cm.).

12. RIVERS. *Panel: Sims* (Armed Constables with Red Clubs), 1970. H: 24" (61 cm.); W: 36" (91.4 cm.).

13. RIVERS. *Panel: Sims* (The Courthouse during Sims' trial), 1970. H: 24" (61 cm.); W: 36" (91.4 cm.).

14. RIVERS. *Panel: Burns being returned to Slavery*, 1970. H: 48" (121.9 cm.); W: 18" (45.7 cm.).

15. RIVERS. *Panel: Burns being returned to Slavery*, 1970. H: 48" (121.9 cm.); W: 72" (182.9 cm.).

16. AUSBY. *Portrait of Sojourner Truth*, 1969. Pastel on paper. H: 25 3/4" (65.4 cm.); W: 19 3/4" (50.2 cm.).

17. AUSBY. *Portrait of Harriet Tubman*, 1969. Pastel on paper. H: 25 3/4" (65.4 cm.); W: 19 3/4" (50.2 cm.).

18. AUSBY. *Madonna and Child*, 1969. Pastel on paper. H: 25 3/4" (65.4 cm.); W: 19 3/4" (50.2 cm.).

19. RIVERS. *The U.S.A. Map* (Southern States and Cotton), 1970. Construction. H: 94" (238.1 cm.); W: 64" (162.5 cm.); D: 37" (94 cm.).

20. RIVERS. *Collage of the Inventor of the Lasting Machine*, 1969-70. Mixed media. H: 17" (43.2 cm.); W: 12" (30.5 cm.).

21. RIVERS. *Large Shoe containing Portrait of the Inventor of the Lasting Machine*, 1970. Construction. H: 35" (88.9 cm.); W: 92" (233 cm); D: 32" (81.3 cm.).

22. RIVERS. *Drawing of Foot*, 1969. Mixed media. H: 17 1/2" (44.4 cm.); W: 12" (30.5 cm.).

23. RIVERS. *Four Sketches of the Lynchings*, 1969. Mixed media. H: 17 1/2" (44.4 cm); W: 12" (30.5 cm.).

24. RIVERS. *Three Cutouts of the Lynchings*, 1969. Mixed media. H: 17 1/2" (44.4 cm.); W: 12" (30.5 cm.).

25. RIVERS. *Drawing for Lynch Figure: Mississippi*, 1970. H: 67" (170.2 cm.); W: 16" (40.6 cm.). Not illustrated.

26. RIVERS. *Drawing for Lynch Figure: Florida*, 1970. H: 78" (198.1 cm.); W: 16" (40.6 cm.). Not illustrated.

27. RIVERS. *Drawing for Lynch Figure: Indiana* (shirt open), 1970. H: 78" (198.1 cm.); W: 17 1/2" (44.4 cm.). Not illustrated.

28. RIVERS. *Drawing for Lynch Figure: Indiana*, 1970. H: 76" (193 cm.); W: 21" (53.3 cm.). Not illustrated.

29. RIVERS. *Caucasian Woman sprawled on a Bed and Eight Figures of Hanged Men on Four Rectangular Boxes*, 1970. Construction.

 A. *Caucasian Woman.* H: 24" (61 cm.); W: 7' (213.4 cm.); D: 6' (182.9 cm.).

 B. *Hanged Man: Florida.* H: 72 " (182.9 cm.); W: 17" (43.2 cm.); D: 5" (12.7 cm.).

 C. *Hanged Man: Mississippi.* H: 68" (172.7 cm.); W: 18 1/4" (46.4 cm.); D: 5" (12.7 cm.).

 D. *Hanged Man: Indiana* (shirt open). H: 79" (200 cm.); W: 18" (45.7 cm.); D: 4" (10.2 cm.).

 E. *Hanged Man: Indiana.* H: 79" (200 cm.); W: 22 1/2" (57.2 cm.); D: 5" (12.7 cm.).

30. RIVERS. *Panel: W. E. B. Du Bois*, 1970. H: 58 1/2" (148.6 cm.); W: 32 1/2" (82.5 cm.).

31. BRADLEY. *Marcus Garvey*, 1970. Construction. H: 43" (109.2 cm.); W: 30" (76.2 cm.); L: 11' 6" (354.9 cm.).

32. RIVERS. *Side View for Ghetto Stoop*, 1969. Pencil on paper. H: 36" (91.4 cm.); W: 24" (61 cm.).

33. RIVERS. *Front View for Ghetto Stoop*, 1969. Pencil on paper. H: 36" (91.4 cm.); W: 24" (61 cm.). Not illustrated.

34. RIVERS. *The Ghetto Stoop*, 1969. Construction. H: 13' 6" (411.6 cm.); W: 10' 4" (315 cm.); D: 8' 10" (269.3 cm.).

35. BOWLING. *Middle Passage*, 1970. Oil on canvas. H: 122" (309.2 cm.); W: 122" (309.2 cm.).

36. RIVERS. *Black Table: Portrait of Frederick Douglass and Malcolm X and Books by Black Authors for Reading*, 1970. Construction. H: 48" (121.9 cm.); W: 44" (111.7 cm.); D: 33" (83.8 cm.).

37. WILLIAMS. *George Washington Carver Crossing the Dupont River May 17, 1954*, 1970. Steel construction, H: 14" (35.6 cm.); W: 48" (121.9 cm.); D: 36" (91.4 cm.). Wood construction, H: 42" (106.7 cm.); W: 60" (152.4 cm.). Linoleum rug, H: 4" (10.1 cm.); W: 96" (243.2 cm.); D: 48" (121.9 cm.). Plaque, H: 3" (7.6 cm.); W: 7 7/8" (20 cm.).

38. JOHNSON. *Over Here, Over There*, 1970. Mixed media. Central painting, H: 84" (212.7 cm.); W: 84" (212.7 cm.); Side pieces, H: 60" (152.4 cm.); W: 48" (121.9 cm.) and H: 84" (212.7 cm.); W: 48" (121.9 cm.).

39. RIVERS. *The Blue Jukebox*, 1970. Construction. H: 87" (220.3 cm.); W: 82 ³/₄" (209.5 cm.); D: 36" (91.4 cm.).

40. RIVERS. *Passing Taxis*, 1970. Construction. H: 78" (198.1 cm.); W: 16' 3 ¹/₂" (496.7 cm.); D: 24" (61 cm.).

41. RIVERS. *Drawing of Hippie Type*. 1970. Mixed media. H: 10 ¹/₄" (26 cm.); W: 5 ¹/₈" (13 cm.).

42. RIVERS. *Portrait of W. E. B. Du Bois*, 1971. Oil and charcoal on canvas. H: 6' (182.9 cm.); W: 4' (122.1 cm.). Not illustrated.

43. RIVERS. *Eldridge Cleaver and Algeria*, 1971. Oil and charcoal on canvas. H: 70" (168 cm); W: 76" (193 cm.).

44. RIVERS. *Imamu Reading* (LeRoi Jones), 1971. Oil and charcoal on canvas. H: 36 ¹/₄" (92 cm.); W: 26" (66 cm.).

45. RIVERS. *Portrait of a Busboy* (Langston Hughes), 1971. Oil and charcoal on shaped canvas. H: 42 ³/₄" (108.5 cm.); W: 35" (89 cm.); D: 3 ³/₄" (9.5 cm.).

46. OVERSTREET. *The New Jemima*, 1964. Construction. H: 102 ¹/₂" (259.7 cm.); W: 61" (154.9 cm.); D: 17" (43.2 cm.).

47. RIVERS. *African Continent and Africans*, 1970. Mixed media. H: 45" (116.8 cm.); W: 36" (91.4 cm.).

48. RIVERS. *African Continent and African*, 1969. Construction. H: 67" (170.2 cm.); W: 64" (162.5 cm.); D: 12 ¹/₂" (31.8 cm.). Not illustrated.

49. RIVERS. *I Like Olympia in Black Face*, 1970. Mixed media. H: 41" (104 cm.); W: 78" (198 cm.); D: 34" (86 cm.).